Endors

Birthing the B

This book is right on time for so many of us in the body who want to write books but never have. I can feel oil on it big time!!!! It deeply touched my heart right from the very beginning. I'm telling you, ITS TIME for this book to *go* forth so other books in people can *come* forth!

I really feel strongly that this book is a KEY being placed in the hands of writers who have books inside of them. It's a key unlocking other books to come up and out of people's hearts. That's what I saw about this book—it is a key.
*—Paula Benne, conference speaker*
*Co-host of the "Shawn and Paula" show.*

If you have a book on the inside of you just waiting to be written, this Holy Ghost handbook is for you. Easily understood, yet rich with practical wisdom and encouragement, Ben Peters gracefully takes you through the insightful and prayerful steps that will help you bring that baby full term and then deliver. I highly recommend it!
*—Georgian Banov*
*President Global Celebration*

Ben Peters is an incredible writer and speaker who brings more than just great writing to those who read his books. Ben has tremendous insights into the heart and ways of God. These insights shed light into practical and easy-to-understand truths. Ben is a true teacher of the Word. I've thoroughly enjoyed his writing and know you'll gain great revelation from this latest book that could release the book inside of you that you've been wanting to write for a long time.
*—Jeff Jansen*
*Global Fire Ministries*

Ben provides first-time writers, a perfect blend of practical and spiritual insights. His book, *Birthing the Book Within You*, is a no-nonsense guide for potential writers who have a burning desire to birth and share what God has shown them.

Ben leads new writers through the rabbit hole maze of authoring and out the other side while whispering in their ear, "You can do all things through Christ who strengthens, guides and directs you." This book shatters the limitations we place on ourselves and opens up the vistas of potential that truly exist in order to fulfill what God is calling us to do.

In keeping with Ben's primary calling, he empowers the Body of Christ to step into what God has called us to fulfill. He brings experience, wisdom, knowledge and faith to the art of writing and the business of publishing.

*—Michael C. Brown*
*Executive Producer, Testimony Pictures*

Ben Peters shares his wisdom gained through experience, right from his heart. This is so encouraging if you have an inspired message from God that you feel needs to be shared. Birthing the Book Within You will be a great assistance. Ben gives you helpful practical strategy with step saving How To tips.

*—Sara E. Trollinger*
*President & Founder, House of Hope*

INSPIRATION AND PRACTICAL HELP
TO PRODUCE YOUR OWN BOOK

# Birthing *the* Book Within You

BEN R. PETERS

Birthing the Book Within You
© 2007 by Ben R. Peters

ISBN: 978-0-9789884-2-5

Unless otherwise indicated, Bible quotations are taken from the New King James Version. Copyright © 1983 by Thomas Nelson, Inc.

Open Heart Ministries
15648 Bombay Blvd.
S. Beloit, IL 61080
www.ohmint.org
benrpeters@juno.com

Cover art used by permission of Robert Bartow
www.bartowimages.com

Book & cover design by Jeff Doles
www.christianbookdesign.com

# Contents

# Preface

As we travel from place to place in ministry, one of the comments I hear the most is, "I know I'm supposed to write a book, but I haven't done it yet." Getting that book from the heart and mind into a beautifully covered work of art seems like such a long, long journey.

I have some good news and some bad news and then some more good news. The first bit of good news is that it really is not that difficult to produce a professional-looking book anymore. The bad news is that even though you have a message from the Lord, and you know your thoughts are anointed and life-changing for anyone who reads them, mainstream publishers probably won't be interested, and most of the potential consumers out there won't be either.

But, as I said, there is still more good news. The good news is that if you are patient, pray a lot, and use God's wisdom, you will touch many lives with your work, and God will put your book into the hands of those He wants to have it. Many little miracles can happen that will bring great joy to your heart. Someone you don't know will write to tell you that your humble effort has transformed their life or their church.

Once a book is released out of your hands and into someone else's hands, many things can happen. The saddest possibility is that your book gets placed in a stack of unread books and never gets read. But often your book will be read with great interest and then passed on to a friend. Sometimes that friend will be from another state or country. They will take your book home and someone else will read it. Before long, you may hear from someone hundreds or thousands of miles away who tells you how much your book has blessed them. They may also want to know more about your ministry, your itinerary, and other books and products you have to offer.

Books journey into places where you could never go and teach people what you might never have had time to teach. Books may contain information and revelation that you have never spoken to a live audience, or they may just be veritable treasure chests of inspiration and revelation. As you read through this little book, please let the Holy Spirit challenge you with the truth that "You CAN do it with His help".

This book is designed to both inspire you and give you practical tips on how to get it done. You CAN write as an oracle of God.

# Chapter One

# Revelation Acceleration

*Y*ou've pictured it in your mind so many times. It's a work of art, but more than that – it's your beautiful gift to the world and to the Kingdom of God. It's filled with creativity, inspiration and revelation, and you just know that almost everyone is going to want to read it. They will surely desire to be impacted by the wisdom, the creativity, the beauty, the anointing and the life-changing truths that your amazing little package contains. Your book will without doubt be on the best-seller list and will revolutionize the church and society in just a short period of time.

But just how and when will this wonderful blessing be revealed and released to the waiting public? How do you get around these mountains of unknown obstacles and impossibilities? Where do you find the time and the help you need to accomplish this glorious task? Is there anyone out there that will believe in you and guide you through this maze without you having to go to college or being required to read a thousand books to learn how to write and publish?

## The Good News

Other than the fact that it does take some work and you may be disappointed at the level of demand for your first book or two, there is a tremendous amount of good news for you, the potential author. If God has put the desire and the message in you, He will help you release it.

## Deliver That Baby Full-Term

If you are pregnant with a message from God, please don't abort it or carry it way past its full term. You want to walk with God and keep in step with Him. There is a time for conception and there is a time for the birthing. Are you ready for the big push? Let's prepare to bring forth the gift that God has given to you to give away. There are souls that He dearly loves who really need the message that He has given to you for them.

## You've Got Mail!

God is downloading fresh revelation, inspiration and creativity at an unprecedented rate. This Heavenly download is invading every aspect of society including media, sports, entertainment, business, government, education and religion. This was foretold by Daniel who said that in the last days "knowledge would increase" (Daniel 12:4). Just as scientific knowledge has obviously increased exponentially, its growth has been clearly paralleled in the world of spiritual information and experience.

We see much evidence of this in our journeys and associations, in the books and magazines we read and in the conferences in which we participate. We cannot keep up with fresh insights that flow from Heaven. It's almost like we could write a new book every day. One man of God prophesied that revelation was my daily bread.

### It's For You, Too.

But God will never give everything to just one or two "special" people or even a small elite group of leaders. He is portioning out revelation to all those who seek Him. God delights in bringing honor to those who have none and confounding the wise with the wisdom released through those who appear to be nobodies in the religious or secular society.

The bottom line is this: If He said that those who speak should speak as oracles of God (I Peter 4:11), then it is clear that it is possible to hear His voice and speak His words. God wouldn't ask us to speak as His oracles if we couldn't first hear His voice. And I'm sure it makes perfect sense to you, as it does to me, that if He can speak through human mouths, then He can write through human hands.

### Writing Versus Speaking

Writing and speaking are clearly just two different ways to express the same thoughts. Their origin is the same. It is only the way that the words and thoughts are delivered that is different. And the good news is that He can use you to deliver His words to man, whether you speak them or write them or both.

God can anoint your written words just as easily as He can anoint your spoken words. If you have ministered to people with your spoken words and experienced an anointing moving through you, that same anointing can flow through you when you write.

## Assisted by Angels

I have heard of preachers who ministered with angels standing by them, clearly visible to various people in the audience. When they would whisper in the ear of the preacher, a strong anointing would be on the words that they spoke. Obviously, these men were speaking as oracles of God in such situations. I believe this happens often with many preachers, but no one in the room has the spiritual vision to see the angels standing there.

In the same way, an angel of revelation or creativity can stand at your side when you write. I was just recently given a very encouraging word that an angel of revelation was with me to give me the words I would share with my readers. It's not because I'm special. I believe it is a common thing. Some men of God I know have actually been visited by what they called "Scribe Angels". They saw these angels with their eyes open like Abraham, Gideon, Peter and Paul and so many others in Scripture. These authors and ministers of the gospel have been given a special mandate to release crucial information for "such a time as this".

## Heaven's Library Rooms

You also may have heard the stories reported by a number

of prophetic speakers, who have seen library rooms in their visits to Heaven. If this is a strange thought or concept to you, please keep an open mind. Many people we know, who are very trustworthy, including children of all ages, have spent quality time in Heavenly places, seeing and hearing amazing things, some of which are impossible for them to describe. If, as Paul declares, we are already seated in Heavenly places, then all it takes is for Him to give us eyes to see what's going on in our new environment.

Some of these visitors to Heaven have reported and written that all the books that God has inspired in the past, as well as books that He will inspire in the future, are already on the bookshelves in Heaven's enormous library rooms. One section is filled with books from the past.

One man who has been there told me that some popular Christian books are absent from the library, while others from more obscure writers hold a prominent place there. The reason some are absent is because they were man's good ideas, but were never ordained by God, even though people may have been blessed by them in various ways.

## Books Yet to be Written

Another huge section is filled with the books that we, who still live on the earth, have been called to write. Just thinking of that fact is very inspiring to me. It's one thing to know that you have a good idea or a special teaching to share with the body of Christ. But it's another thing to realize that you have a mandate from God to release and transfer that creativity into a book that is already sitting on the bookshelves in Heaven. You can now bring a copy of that book to earth and cause it to be placed on bookshelves for your earthly brothers and sisters to read.

Now, it's not about me and my book and how successful it will be. It's not about how many people will read it and think about how great a writer or how wise a teacher I am. It is clearly about His Kingdom, His body, His church and His bride. It's about a mandate, a responsibility, a privilege and an incredible joy.

It's not work anymore, even though it may take much energy and dedication. Rather it is something that is energized by love for Jesus and His Kingdom. It is a partnering with Him to get His ideas into the minds of His children, so that they might be renewed and transformed according to His purpose and plan.

I have now become part of God's team, doing my part to make Him successful by accomplishing His goals on earth, using the gifts and talents that He has given me, rather than burying them in the dirt. I have the honor of knowing that some day He will say, "Well done, good and faithful servant."

## Help Wanted – Scribes

Job Description: Take dictation from the Boss and publish it for the world to read.

God has plans to release an incredible volume of knowledge, wisdom, understanding and revelation of all kinds. He will release scientific technology, medical breakthroughs, nutritional wonders and understanding of creation and the universe. He will further enhance communication technology and bring about a radical transformation of the entire world in a very short period of time.

What excites God the most is the Truth that sets men free being released in much greater clarity to the entire body of Christ in these strategic days. It will be truth that activates a sleeping church and empowers her to rise up and conquer. She will be motivated to go out to the over-ripe harvest fields and quickly gather the precious souls that will become a part of His beautiful bride.

With all this information, wisdom, understanding and divine strategy to be released, God is looking for willing scribes. He knows exactly who has been given the writing gifts and He is prompting some of them even as they are reading these lines. He is saying, "You've heard my voice – you know I've called you. Will you let me use you for my purposes and plans? You CAN do it! I will help you every step of the way. Let's get started, and together we'll do it one step at a time."

*Chapter Two*

# It's Not So Hard Anymore

There is no argument against the statement that writing a book has never been easier. Technology, especially the computer, has changed everything today.

## Remembering the Old Methods of Writing

While in college and university, I had to write many papers and finally a master's thesis. What a chore that was, compared to the way we do it today. We had our mechanical typewriters then, before the electric ones came out. You didn't write your first drafts on the typewriter, because it was too difficult to change and move things around or correct mistakes. If you did, you had to double or triple space so you could write new thoughts you wanted to add in the space between the lines.

If you made mistakes in your final draft, (which most college students do frequently, even with several years of typing classes) you had to use some form of eraser that would rip the page up a bit. Whiteout later became popular and a variety of correction tapes became available as well. Bottom line, fixing mistakes was very difficult and taking out a paragraph or moving it after you had finished the document was not possible without redoing much of the project.

Writing a whole book on a typewriter would have been a major task, as was my master's thesis. Perhaps that's why it took me long past my graduation date to finally get it done. Actually, there really were several other bigger factors, but writing a master's thesis then was certainly a much greater task than it is today.

## Remembering the Old Methods of Printing

When I was a teenager, my dad took over his father-in-law's printing shop. It featured a big old linotype and a huge press that printed newsprint-sized sheets. It also had a small hand press, which I was allowed to run, and several other small machines such as folders, paper cutters and electric staplers. We printed numerous Christian books, newspapers, tracts and flyers, etc., most of them in German. We exported them to other countries from our community in Coaldale, Alberta, Canada.

What a job it was to get a book into print. The linotype had a pot to melt lead. It also had movable letter molds that fell into a chamber when you struck a key on the unique keyboard. You'd line up the letter molds and spacers would expand to fill up the row. When you had the molds ready you would allow the molten lead to fill the molds and you would end up with lead type that had letters protruding out. When this type was put together on a board and properly tightened into place, you could put the whole thing into the press. Then the ink rollers would roll over the type, which of course had to be backwards, or a mirror image of the final product. After the rollers had inked the lead, a sheet of paper would be pressed against the letters and you would have a printed page. The term press must have come from the fact that the paper is pressed against the type.

## The Offset Press

I later was trained to print on a couple of different offset presses. They didn't require the lead type, which is now antiquated, but they involved taking photos off a printed page and burning the image onto a master sheet, which was in turn put on a drum. Chemical solutions were applied to the master sheet, ink rollers would roll over it, and the ink would only stick to where the image had been made. The paper was then pressed against the master sheet, and finally you had a printed copy on a sheet of paper.

My frustration with the offset presses was getting the right amount of chemical solutions and the right amount of ink to make a quality job. Too much chemical solution meant you needed more ink released; however, if the ink then got too dark, you needed more chemicals. It was easier to add than subtract both entities, and it was always a challenge to get it right.

As computers and digital technology exploded on the scene in our society, both writing and printing changed dramatically.

Now you can even find software that will type what you say without you having to use the keyboard. I haven't used that myself, but if you don't type very well, you might want to check out that type of software at your nearest computer tech store.

## Computer Software Makes Writing Much Easier

There are many programs that help a writer get things done, but one of the most popular is Microsoft Word. My first laptop came with it, but when I bought the one I'm using today, I had to pay extra to have it installed. But I sure wouldn't want to live without it, unless something better comes out that everyone uses. It's important to use a program that formatters and editors also use, so you can transfer your manuscripts to them by email.

## Advantages of Programs like Microsoft Word

### A. Spelling

Many potential writers worry about their poor spelling ability. While no program is foolproof, the vast majority of your spelling mistakes will be taken care of by these programs. With Word, your misspelled word may just self-correct, like the word, "misspelled" just did. I spelled it with a single "s" rather than a double "s". I was just testing the program, of course. If your boo-boo does not self-correct, your smarter-than-you program will normally place a squiggly red line under your misspelled word.

## B. Grammar Check

If your sentences are not grammatically correct, your program may underline that section with a green line to alert you to a problem. With a right click of the mouse on the underlined text, you can read what it has to say about your improper use of the English language.

## C. Formatting

With a little coaching, you can learn how to format your writing with bullet points and automatic numbering, etc. There are many of these options that I have never even learned to use, but being practical, I tend to not explore as much as I should, wanting instead to get my job done, using the tools I already know how to use.

## D. Tools

Microsoft Word has a tab called tools. The way I use this the most is to check how many words I have written. I'm usually looking for a book that is long enough to be a book, but not so long that it discourages people from reading the whole thing.

The word count is a wonderful tool to figure out how many book pages I have written. I check my previous books and figure out how many words make a 100 page book. For me it takes just over 25,000 words to fill one hundred pages in my books. That's about 250 words per book page, which is not the same as your computer page. This book will be shorter to keep it more user-friendly.

Other tools include auto-correct options, shared work

space, voice recognition, and many other options. Those who have a curious mind can get very creative and even artistic.

### E. Editing

By far the most useful item on your computer is the edit function, which includes, cut and paste, copy and paste, highlight, delete, etc. The ability to change things in your document, by moving your curser and backspacing to delete or to simply insert additional information, is a revolutionary improvement over the old typewriters I used in college.

In addition, you can decide to highlight a passage after it is written. You can choose to underline, put in italics and/or use bold print. You can change the font size and the style of print from many interesting choices. You can insert pictures or icons or whatever you want if you learn how to use the program.

## Print on Demand Digital Printing is a Major Breakthrough

If you are not very famous and no major publishing company is pursuing you with a contract to write a book, you probably don't want to buy several thousand books on the first printing. However, that is what was required to print a book just a few years ago, and you would have had to put out thousands of dollars just to get started. Then you would have to find a place to store those thousands of books, with the hope that someone would be willing to buy them from you someday.

I don't have to understand how they do it, but today digital printing companies, who do print on demand, will print one book for you after they have it in their computers. That's right! They will print just one book, send it to you, and charge you the price of one book plus shipping. Of course, you will probably order more than one book at a time, but any option is now available to you.

The setup and printing charges are very reasonable, and you don't have to find a publisher that believes your book will be successful. You just have to believe that God has given you a book and He will use it for His glory.

God has given me great favor, and for just a few hundred dollars, I have my book formatted, cover designed and submitted to the printers. Before that, a wonderful friend (and professional proofreader) goes through the manuscript with a fine-toothed comb. The whole process takes only a few weeks once I have finished the manuscript and chosen a cover picture. Before long, I have a beautiful brand new book in my hands.

In case you feel that your book is so good that a big publisher will want to print it and promote it everywhere, you should become aware of the facts. I was recently informed that traditional publishers reject 95% of all manuscripts submitted to them. The 5% that they accept are usually the ones they pursued in the first place – books by authors whose names are recognized by the hundreds of thousands of people in the marketplace.

In my own experience, my first big book (still my only book over 200 pages), *Signs and Wonders – To Seek or Not to Seek*, was going to be a national best-seller. I had worked hard on it, done lots of research, and miraculously gotten a foreword by well-known prophet, Bill Hamon. I had another dozen or so endorsements by pastors and ministry leaders.

In addition to that, Bill Hamon was recommending my book to his own publisher. I was quite excited and felt I was on the way to becoming a famous author. But, not so fast! From that point on, everything dragged on and on. I got the manuscript quickly to the editor, but I didn't hear back from him for some time. After several attempts to communicate, I learned that he had not even looked at it yet.

After about a year, and a little pestering from me, the editor finally admitted that they had too many other priorities to publish my book any time in the near future. That was when I found a self-publishing, print-on-demand company. I published several books through them, before I discovered that a friend of mine was doing the same thing for himself that this publishing company was doing for me.

The result was that for a fraction of the cost, and a fraction of the time, I had him do my formatting, cover and other little details. Soon it was only taking weeks instead of months or years to get a book into print. That is how I was able to produce four new books in less that one year.

It clearly has never been this easy to write and produce a finished copy of a brand new book. But we don't just want to write and produce a book for the sake of doing it. We want to produce something that will be a blessing to many people. We want a book that will impact our world. We want to write God's book for Him.

That must include some amount of work and organization.

It will require some preparation and structure. We can't just write and write without chapters, titles and sub-titles. How do we organize our thoughts and write that book that God called us to birth?

Our next chapter will deal with the question just asked. We will take a closer look at the process of preparation and organization. We will share some strategic tips to help you get your thoughts on paper in such a way that people will not want to stop reading, once they get started. Are you ready for the next step? Don't quit on me now! Let's move on.

# Chapter Three

# Preparation & Organization

### Preparation for a Journey

Although writing a book may be a new journey or venture for you, reading your book must also become a new and exciting journey for your readers. Even though you may have all the greatest information in the world, information alone will not get many people excited. What people want is an adventure.

You may be writing a different type of book than I have written. It may be a fiction novel, which is almost always adventurous, or it may be a book of poetry or something totally different, but you want your reader to feel like they are being guided into a new and exciting world in which surprises and adventure lurk at every turn.

Like network news commentators, you want your readers to be anticipating what comes next so they don't "change that channel during the commercial". Many Christian book readers have several books they hope to read, but have a limited amount of time to spend reading them. They have become "picky" consumers, and they don't want to waste their time reading something that seems to be boring at first impression.

## Defining Success as an Author

I feel successful as an author if the reader not only decides the book is worth buying and begins reading it, but he or she actually reads it from cover to cover. One of the best compliments I received was from a lady, who was given my book, *With Me*, and reluctantly read it. She told me that she was only upset that it wasn't any longer. She stayed interested until the end and wanted more. That's the response you want from your readers.

If you are writing fiction, you can more easily hold your readers attention, because they become emotionally involved with the characters in the story and want to see how the problems they have encountered in your plot are resolved. But with a teaching book, such as I usually write, it's not that easy. I can't say that I have always consciously tried to keep baiting the reader to keep him or her reading one more chapter. I have just instinctively let people know what was coming, as a natural way to keep them interested.

If you keep this concept in mind that you are guiding your readers on a journey of adventure and discovery, you will learn to ask the right questions, such as, "Have I told them enough so far to keep them excited, while letting them know that something even better is waiting for them in the next chapter?" Or ask yourself, "Have I written too many irrelevant details that will bore the reader?"

## Turnoffs for Today's Busy Readers

Today's busy book consumers do not want your preaching, your soapbox dissertations, useless information or needless repetition. If they want to review, they can go back to where they read it the first time. It's not like TV, where if you miss it, you might not have another chance to see it again. They want the lean meat without the bones and fat.

Readers are easily turned off by anything that does not meet some need in their heart or mind. The author must learn to streamline his message to get right to the point, and if he or she has a target audience, he must know what the needs are of that audience.

If the target audience is mothers of pre-school children, you don't want to write too much about your ideas on nuclear physics or football. Instead, you might want to talk about how they can make time to get alone with God or keep a journal, in spite of their hectic and stressful schedule.

## Meeting Your Readers Needs

The people holding your book in their hands want to read something they have not previously known. And they want something that has an easy and practical application in their life. They want the light to go on in their mind or heart. They want to all of a sudden feel like they understand something clearly for the first time.

Readers need to have something to say, "WOW!" about. Throughout their journey through your book, they should repeatedly encounter that "WOW!" And with every "WOW!" there should be a clue that causes them to anticipate the next "WOW!"

## Lead them to the Treasure

Like the movie, "National Treasure", your book can lead your reader, clue by clue, to a tremendous treasure. Not all books can or need to build to a final climax in the last chapter, but it is a technique that should be employed whenever possible.

The strategy in doing this is to give another clue, or piece of information, with each chapter. Each chapter can build on the knowledge revealed in the previous chapter. But the reader must be aware that the real treasure has not yet been revealed. The greatest revelation should be released near the end of the book. After that, you need to wrap up quickly so your final thoughts don't become anti-climatic.

The treasure that you share in the high point of your book should hopefully be a powerful revelation from God that will change the way people think and behave. The truth you uncover for them should be something that they can now believe applies to them personally. It will be a revelation they can use to change their world.

## Other Styles or Types of Writing

Another type of book may present the most important truth right at the beginning. If the book is written with God's wisdom, this strategy will not leave the reader disinterested in the rest of the book. Rather, it will only make him or her more eager than ever to find out what you have to say.

## A. Up Front Thesis

You might begin your book with a statement or thesis that shocks the reader or stirs up a controversial subject. The rest of the book will step by step prove your point. But you still must make each chapter an adventure, and you need to keep your readers aware that they are on a journey of discovery and there is still a lot they need to know. They should still feel that the best is yet to come, which will be experienced if they keep reading.

## B. "How To" Books

Other books, like this one, are written for the purpose of instructing and inspiring readers to accomplish something they want to do. People with no interest in writing, will probably never buy or read this book. I have a specific target audience. You, the reader, already have an interest in the subject at hand, or you would never have read to this point.

What will keep you interested in reading past this point is the awareness that you don't yet have enough information to fulfill your dream of having your own book in your hands and in the hands of thousands of readers. So far you have been encouraged that you can write that book. You have been made aware that your book may have already been authorized in Heaven and all of Heaven is anticipating its release through you.

If you have read the table of contents, you know there is valuable information still to come. And before this chapter is over, you will be reminded that there are important nuggets of information awaiting your discovery.

## Interesting Titles

The ideas presented next will apply to both your book title and to your chapter titles. You only need one book title, but it is probably more important than all your chapter titles combined. However, if you have the right book title and also have chapter titles that captivate attention, you have a much better chance of changing the casual book browser into a serious book buyer.

I like to give titles that catch people's interest as soon as they read them. I had a chance to develop this gift one year, when I wrote the sports news for a small-town weekly newspaper while pastoring a small town church. Sports news is one area that allows writers and editors to use their imagination to create interest. Playing on words or "punning" is widely practiced and you can use creativity to your heart's content.

Whether or not you have experience in writing catchy titles, God can inspire you and increase your creativity to a whole new level. Let's look at some possibilities and examples.

## A. Words that Have Rhyme or Rhythm

Chapter One of this book is titled, "Revelation Acceleration". This is an example of both rhythm and rhyme. If you read it like a "rapper" might say it, you might read it like

"Re-va-LA-tion Ac-cel-a-RA-tion". Most readers won't get the full impact, but it still has a catchy sound, and it still provokes interest.

## B. Interesting and Thought-Provoking Statements

Chapter Two is titled "It's Not So Hard Anymore." This is a statement that tells the reader something that makes him or her ask the question, "Why?" Obviously, the second chapter is going to explain why it's not so hard anymore. This is something you want to know if you want to write a book, and you were encouraged to read and find out why your "mountain" is now just a big "molehill".

My book, *Resurrection – A Manual for Raising the Dead*, catches people's attention immediately. Who would presume to write a manual for raising the dead? People will pick up the book just to see if you are serious or not. Of course, some people ask if I've ever raised the dead. I usually reply, "Thousands", and sometimes I explain how that is true.

Another book was titled, *Catching Up to the Third World*. It catches people's attention right away, because we assume the "Third World" is behind us in "First World" nations.

## C. Titles that Promise Important and Helpful Information

The third chapter of this book, which you are now reading, is titled "Preparation and Organization". Many potential writers ask me the questions that I am trying to address in this chapter. They have many ideas they want to communicate, but struggle to organize them into logical chapter divisions.

We still have a lot of ground to cover at this point in the chapter to fulfill the promise made by the title, but being a good "Promise Keeper", I intend to keep that promise.

## D. Titles that Borrow from a Well-known Phrase

My first professionally published book was titled *Signs and Wonders – To Seek or Not to Seek*. Most people have heard the quote from Shakespeare, "To be or not to be, that is the question." "To seek or not to seek", borrows from the famous line and rings a familiar chord in the reader's mind.

One chapter in my book, *With Me*, is titled "No Fear Here". Short titles or headings are always best if you can find a two-word or three-word phrase that works. "No fear here" borrows from the popular phrase "No Fear" and uses the rhyming word "here" for added "catchiness". By the way, you can make up new words like "catchiness" if you put them in quotation marks. Then the "Microsoft Word" program won't put a big squiggly red mark under them.

Maybe the most attention-catching title I've written that borrows from a well-known phrase is *Go Ahead, Be so Emotional*. Everyone has heard people say to someone, "Don't be so emotional." Again, there is a bit of a shock effect and people often laugh when they read it and say, "This one's for me!"

## E. Titles that Indicate a Mystery

Another book I wrote was given the title, *God's Favorite Number*. Most kids have favorite colors and numbers. I don't know what God's favorite color is, but I do know what His favorite number is. Aren't you curious about what that number might be? You're probably guessing right now, but chances are you are wrong like most people who guess. Hopefully, you'll go out and buy the book.

### Shoot the Bunny Before You Start

Readers want to be able to follow a clear path to the treasure you are leading them to. They don't want to be led down dozens of dead-end bunny trails on the way to the treasure. Determine to kill the bunny before you follow it down the path of confusion.

Confusion is your enemy. Mystery is your friend. There is a difference. Confusion is when it appears that you, their supposed leader, don't know where you are going. Mystery is when they know that you know where you are going, but they have to keep reading if they want to actually find out where you are going.

You must always remain aware that writing is different than preaching. Frequent repetition and bunny trails can be useful at times in preaching, but they should be avoided in writing. You want your book to be "lean meat" full of "protein" to build readers up without attaching any unnecessary baggage to their lives.

Usually, when you preach, people are too self-conscious to just get up and leave if they find you boring. However, when they are reading your book in the privacy of their own home, they won't hesitate to put it down and never pick it back up again. That's what you want to avoid.

## Organize your Thoughts and Ideas into Common Elements

### A. Chronologically

You may be writing a story, testimony or biography. Your chapter divisions could relate to different periods of time in the life of your subject. One technique is to start with one of the most interesting or exciting moments or events, where you tell some, but not all of the story. Then back up to tell the readers how your hero or heroine got to that point in their life. After that, you can finish the story you started at the beginning.

### B. Logically

We can also organize thoughts logically, building from foundation to walls, to ceilings, to windows and doors, to the exterior and interior decorating. You can present the basic foundational truths, such as "Saved by Grace". Then you can add the life of intimacy and heart and soul fulfillment (walls and ceilings). After that you can teach on spiritual gifts and ministries (the visible decoration) that flow out of intimacy.

Having an outline with "Main Topics" and "Sub-Topics" is a very wise way to organize your ideas. Main topics will be the key points in your book. Sub-topics will fill in the most significant details. Other details can be added under the sub-topics.

### C. By Other Subject Categories

Your book may be more of an informational book, such

as a gardening guide. You can then divide your information into various types of plants with common characteristics. Or you could write a cook book and divide your chapters into various types of food.

This type of book would be more of a resource book, rather than the kind that people should read from start to finish in the order it was written. It should be well-organized so that people can find the information they need with the least amount of effort.

## Keep the "Bite-Sized" Concept in Mind

Books written even fifty to one hundred years ago were much different than books today. People were not inundated with electronic media. They had little entertainment and few sources of information. People could handle a lot of information in a book, and were not in such a hurry to get to the main point.

Today, however, readers just do not have the time, and they have very little patience for a book with too many insignificant details. They want "bite-sized" nuggets, not a whole "side of beef".

## Keep your Paragraphs Short

I learned this bit of wisdom while writing for the newspaper. A long paragraph discourages readers from wanting to read the whole thing. A paragraph of two or three medium length sentences looks like something they can handle.

Your reader may be getting ready to go to bed, but he or she can read one more paragraph, or even two, if the paragraphs are short enough. It's the old adage, "Take two – they're small."

## Break up Your Pages with Sub-Titles

I am using this technique to the extreme in this book as an example to you. The logic behind this is similar to what we just shared above. When people see a whole page or two of boring-looking small print with no breaks in the pages, they get subconsciously discouraged from reading it.

Remember when you couldn't read at all. You looked at books with pictures. Words were boring, because you couldn't read them. Today, pages without built-in breaks appear boring to most readers. They want that bite-sized look.

When your reader sees the sub-topics highlighted with short paragraphs following, he or she gets motivated to read some more. The bold print catches their attention, and it is actually like a short ad with information about what is coming up next.

In other words, you are advertising your next few paragraphs. You want to sell the reader on the importance of reading what is coming. Because of the disposition of modern readers, many readers today skim or read here and there. You won't keep them reading if you don't keep letting them know what you are preparing to reveal to them.

We have discussed some ideas on how to organize and prepare to write. Now let's look at the next step – starting to write. We can do this! God is with us.

*Chapter Four*

# It's Time to Write Your Book

## Let God Impart a Spirit of Creativity and Focus

Remember, you are writing the book that God wants you to write. Let Him take the pressure – He CAN handle it! Use the guidelines and instructions already given to help you through the process, but pray continually for God's help and wisdom. Don't let my rules or anyone else's rules take away your sense of freedom to be creative.

Above all, pray for His anointing, the anointing of a "ready writer" who has a message from God to write for others to read. Ask Him to protect the message from anything that would confuse or distract the reader from the message He has given you to write. But ask Him to give you the ability to make the message as exciting and captivating as possible.

Keep in mind that no matter how great your information

is, if no one reads it, you will not be making any impact or changing your world. You need to pray for the wisdom of God to make the book you are writing for Him as attractive to the reader as possible. You want people not only to acquire and start reading the book, but you want them to be motivated throughout the book to read it completely.

## Your Best Publicity Tool

There are many ways to promote your book. There are agencies that you can pay to advertise and publicize the book for you. You can advertise on radio and TV programs, you can do book signings at bookstores, or you can advertise in various publications at significant expense. All these methods can help your book become known and read.

But there is one key factor that will make a bigger difference than all of the above in the long run. That factor is the impact that your book has on each individual reader who does read it. If your readers are not impacted or impressed by your book, then they will not recommend it to anyone else. You will have to pay for all your advertising, while others benefit and profit from "word-of-mouth" advertising.

On the other hand, one person who is impacted by your book can influence many more people to get your book. If it is really revolutionary and touches a nerve in society or the Kingdom of God, you may find your book receiving free advertisement over TV and radio talk shows, or it may be written up and quoted in newspaper and magazine articles.

In other words, the content of your book and the manner in which it is presented are two very important keys for getting your book read by multitudes people. As we mentioned above, if you get your message from Heaven, write with a flow of Holy Spirit anointing, and then do your best to use God's wisdom and skill to put it all together, you will have the potential to impact the greatest number of people. When you have completed such a book, you will also maximize the advertising dollars that you do spend to let people know about your book.

## Knowing Your Purpose for Writing

I feel compelled to add this exhortation. How passionate do you feel about the book you are writing? Will you be content with the fact that you wrote a book and had it published or printed? Is this book something that you want to do just so you can feel like you have accomplished something and can say you are an author? Or do you have a passion to touch people's lives, to transform the church and/or society in general?

If you just want a book in your name, that's easy. If you have a little cash to spare, anyone can self-publish a book these days. And there's nothing wrong with fulfilling a dream to be an author, without trying to change the world. However, if your passion is to impact your world in a radical way, and to bring life or hope to people whose lives can be changed by your revelation, then everything we have been discussing is important to you.

Of course, God can superimpose His own hand over yours, and He can dictate every word to you as you write. That would, without a doubt, produce the perfect book. But the chances are that He will allow you to express His thoughts through your personality and giftings, and through some concentrated effort.

It will take some work on your part, and if you want to produce something that will bless His Kingdom, you don't want to turn people off because you haven't done your homework or paid attention to important details. Let's look at some of the ways you can assure that your book will have that extra spark that will set it apart from books that are just man's good ideas.

## Spend Extra Time in the Word and Meditation

Pray as you read and study God's Word. Let Him know that you are dependent on Him for revelation, and your book is for His Kingdom and His children. You want to feed them with something they can use that will bless their journey and help them to fulfill their destiny.

As you read and pray while you are reading, revelation and creativity will flow. The "logos" will become the "rhema", and you will be amazed by His willingness to help you write His book for Him.

## Worship While You Prepare and While You Write

The best way to hear from God, along with reading His Word, is to worship. He does inhabit our praise and worship. His presence comes and with His presence comes His anointing. A writing anointing can come as easily as a speaking anointing.

Because it's kind of hard to sing or play an instrument while you write, it would be a good idea to have some soft worship music in the background. You can worship with your spirit along with the music while you meditate and receive creativity for your book. If soft music puts you to sleep and you are writing an action novel, then use something with more intensity that will put you in the mood and open you up to the kind of Spirit of creativity that you need.

## Be Prepared for Fresh Revelation and Creativity

While you write in an attitude and atmosphere of worship, you may find yourself writing thoughts and ideas that you have never considered before. You can get into a flow that will amaze you later when you read what you have written.

You do want to follow your outline, but be prepared for the extra ideas or illustrations that will drop into your mind as you write. Even after you have organized all your thoughts into the proper compartments, God will mess with you like He does with me, whether I'm preaching or writing. He always gives something last minute or while I'm in the process.

When I read what I've written later, I am often amazed. "Wow!" I say to myself, "I've never heard that before! That's a really great point. I wish I had thought of that." I truly get blown away, because there are things I've written that I've never preached, because I forgot the revelation shortly after I wrote it.

## Be Aware of Other Sources of Revelation and Inspiration

God does give grace to the humble. Don't think you already know it all regarding your subject matter. God will use people around you to drop nuggets in your path if you are looking for them and are willing to listen to others.

Don't be surprised if He uses a child or someone with little education or social standing to spark creativity in you. At the same time, take in everything you can from the wisdom of leaders that you know and respect. It may amaze you how often people will touch on your subject of interest while you are preparing and writing your book.

You won't just parrot what they have said, but you can quote them if you want. The greatest blessing will be that what they say will trigger another question, and the answer to that question will be a fresh revelation. I have had that happen to me so many times and through many different speakers and teachers.

## Starting the First Chapter

You only have one chance to get it right from the get-go. Your first chapter, your first paragraph and your first sentence should be designed to lock your reader into the idea that this book is a must read.

One great way to get good ideas is simply to read other books and see how they caught your attention with their first words. I just looked back to see how I started chapter one in this book. "Not bad!" I said to myself. If you go back to read it, I think you'll find that it got your attention.

One common method of grabbing the reader's attention is to begin with a dramatic story. If you are writing a novel, the whole book is a story. However, if you are writing teaching books as I do, you can still start with a story illustrating the need for the information that is about to be read.

Another technique is to ask a very thought-provoking question that the reader will want answered. If you are writing about the baptism in the Holy Spirit, you might begin the book by asking the questions, "Can you be filled with the Holy Spirit without speaking in tongues? Is the gift of tongues the only true evidence that you have been baptized in the Holy Spirit?"

For most Pentecostals and Charismatics, these questions would spark their interest, and they would want to know what you had to say, even if they already had a strong opinion on the subject. They might be ready to argue with you in their minds, but they would still want to know your opinion.

## First Chapter Content

Guard against saying too much in the first chapter. Let Chapter One be a concise introduction to the whole book. You don't want to give too much detail in your first few pages. Don't give your reader mental or emotional indigestion before he or she gets to Chapter Two.

By keeping your first chapter lean, you will be creating a mood and setting a perceived precedent that you won't be wordy, redundant or unsure of where you are going. Get to the point of what your book is going to be about. Give them some clues, but don't spill the beans yet.

Let Chapter One give an example or two of the amazing information that you are about to release, but let some of the chapter be devoted to promoting the revelations that are coming in future chapters. If today's reader actually begins Chapter Two, you have already accomplished something significant.

## Main Body of Your Book

Hopefully, because of the anointing on your writing and the wisdom you have shared, your reader is still reading after Chapter One and you have more good food to serve them. Now you are ready to start building the main infrastructure of your book.

The introduction to the second chapter, and every succeeding chapter, should follow the same principles that we suggested you should use for the entire first chapter. In other words, give a very concise statement, which clues your readers into what's in store for them as they read this chapter.

Try to be careful to keep each chapter on track. If you are studying Old Testament references to father/son relationships, resist the temptation to discuss a couple of New Testament references. If you are telling a story or writing a biography, let each chapter focus on a particular topic or period in the person's life.

## Suggestions for Writing Biographies or Autobiographies

As mentioned earlier, you can organize a person's history by time periods or by aspects of personality or character. For instance, you could start with early childhood, then discuss the person's youth, young adulthood, middle age and finish with their life as a senior citizen.

Or you could focus one chapter on a character quality such as determination, and then look at another quality such as loyalty. You could focus one chapter on crises he or she had to deal with and another on major accomplishments in his or her life. This would involve stories from their childhood to their death, if they have passed away.

You could combine both types of organization, but you should focus on only one category in each chapter. The reader gains confidence in you as a writer if you come across as organized rather than scattered.

## Your Final Chapter – Concluding Your Treasure Hunt

Depending on the type and style of your book, you can make the final chapter the climax or just a quick wrap-up and review. If your climax comes in the second-to-the-last chapter, then keep the final chapter very short and concise. You are simply tying up loose ends and reminding the readers what they have learned in the book.

If the last chapter contains your climax, and you don't need an extra chapter to wrap up loose ends, then keep your subject matter as to-the-point as possible. The reader is anxious for everything to come together. He or she is probably tired of details and wants to get to the "big" point of the book. Don't let him or her down. Reward your readers with the prize you have promised them for reading your book.

### Final Statement

It's hard to say which is more important, the opening statement or the final statement of your book. Both are critically important in my opinion. The opening statement should encourage the reader to read your book, but the final statement should leave the reader with the feeling that your book was well worth reading and worth telling someone else about.

The final statement should capture both the factual information and the emotional impact of your book. It should express your heart and passion for the things you have been communicating to your readers.

Ask the Holy Spirit to inspire you with the exact words He wants to say that will stay with your readers. If you are writing as an "oracle of God", this will happen rather naturally. Personally, I have felt a special anointing on many of my final statements that I know had to be God.

Once we have completed the content, we can work on some of the "accessories" that give your book a more professional feel and provide helpful information for your reader. Let's examine several of these "accessories" in the next chapter.

## Chapter Five

# Accessorizing Your Book

There are numerous parts of books that can be included, depending on your type of book and how formal or informal you want it to be. I have used most of them at least once, and some of them I have used quite consistently. Let's take a little look at some of the possibilities.

### The Foreword

First of all, please note the spelling. It's different than going "forward". This is a "word" that comes "before" – thus the word, "foreword".

A foreword is a great option if you have someone in your circle of friends who has some name recognition (especially if you don't). Hopefully, this friend will be willing to go to bat for you. You might want to ask the potential foreword writer long before you finish your manuscript if he or she would be willing to read and possibly endorse it. If this friend is well known, he or she is probably very busy, and won't feel taken advantage of if given enough notice.

If you are blessed with that special person who has name recognition, his or her name can be written boldly on the front cover. You can make the print of their name as big as your own so that potential readers will easily notice it. It will say, "FOREWORD BY_____". Hopefully the browsing customer will open the book to see what your friend has to say about you and your book.

Often the writer of the foreword can say very nice and positive things about you and your book that you would not be comfortable saying yourself. This can become extremely beneficial to you, the author. God can lead you in this effort just as easily as He can anoint your book.

I know of one writer, who previously had little or no name recognition, but let a well-known friend read her manuscript. He got quite enthused about it and wrote a very strong foreword for her. Soon a portion of it was being published on an email list reaching tens of thousands of readers. Before she had published her book she had over two thousand orders and had to print them up at Kinko's to fill the orders.

Through a miraculous word of knowledge coming via a dear elderly saint from Calgary, Alberta, Bishop Bill Hamon blessed me with a foreword, as I reported earlier. Without knowing me personally, he read my manuscript and wrote the foreword, partly based on the word of knowledge given by our dear friend, Zona. She was given his name through a supernatural word of knowledge, without knowing who he was. When we were talking about getting a foreword for this book, which she loved, she said, "Does the name H-A-M-O-N mean anything to you?"

I said, "Don't you know Bill Hamon?"

She said, "I don't think so. But if I heard the name I would have spelled it: H-A-M-M-O-N-D."

I told her that I had sent him a manuscript and another one to Peter Wagner, who had already declined writing a foreword. It had been about six weeks, and I hadn't heard a thing from Bishop Hamon.

I immediately called the office of Christian International, Bill Hamon's ministry, and told the story. They said he had been overseas all summer but would be back in ten days. Ten days later I called again. Bill had stopped in the office, but had not seen the manuscript yet.

I decided to let it go and see what would happen. Three days later I got a personal call from Bishop Hamon. He said he had read the book, liked it, and had already written the foreword, which I would receive that day by email. He chatted with me for almost half an hour. It really made my day. Today, all of my books have more credibility, just because of that one foreword.

Because of my haste to get books finished and available for our upcoming conferences, I often forgo seeking a foreword. But as you can see from the two stories above, God can really bless and lead you in this endeavor. Ask the Lord if He has someone in mind that can give your book the extra appeal that attracts more readers.

Remember, your book can be the most wonderful revelation,

but if no one reads it, you have wasted your time writing it. A foreword by the right person can make a huge difference.

## Endorsements

Books seldom have more than one foreword, but they often have numerous endorsements. A foreword will usually be one to three pages in length, but endorsements can be as short as one phrase, such as "A must read!"

The normal endorsement will be a paragraph or two, but again the key is name recognition or an official title such as, president or senior pastor, etc., but don't limit your possibilities. Sometimes, I like to include nameless, faceless people to give the "normal person" appeal. For my book "Go Ahead, Be So Emotional", I got endorsements from three "emotional" and unknown people that everyone who might find this book appealing could relate to.

## Preface

You, the author, are the one to write this introduction to your book. It could also be one to three pages in length.

The preface can contain information that would be distracting in the main part of the book. It can give disclaimers and explanations that wouldn't be appropriate later. It can also contain added information that will prepare the reader for what is coming. It can even update what was written in a previous publication of the same book.

Basically, you can say whatever you want in the preface to help prepare your readers for what is coming, and you have the liberty to be a little more candid and personal, since it is not the main part of the book. Many readers will actually skip the preface, in their hurry to get to the meat. You might want to reward those who do read it with a bit of "juicy" information that would be more personal and private than the rest of the book.

## Acknowledgements

If certain people helped you in a significant way in getting your book completed, it is appropriate to write a paragraph or two acknowledging their contributions. In addition to those who actually added something to the book, you can acknowledge family members who sacrificed time with you so that you could focus on writing your book.

You can always acknowledge a spouse for moral support and for putting up with you through the process. You can acknowledge the Holy Spirit for the inspiration, etc. And it would be good to acknowledge other men and women of God who have encouraged you with their own teachings and examples that led you to produce what you have written in your book.

## Dedication

If you would particularly like to honor any individual or group of people, you can add a dedication paragraph or two. The dedication doesn't necessarily include the person or group of people who helped you write the book directly. The dedication is directed to people you highly admire, people who have inspired you with their own lives. They are people who have made a major difference in your life, and you want to take this opportunity to let them know how blessed you are by them.

## Table of Contents

Your table of contents lists your chapter titles and the page numbers. It also lists the other items – the accessories that you are adding to the book. Since you won't know what pages your chapters will start on in your book, you can leave that item with whoever formats your book.

## Prologues and Epilogues

A prologue is placed before the main body of the book and gives insight as to what has happened prior to the release of the book. It could be the second book in a series for instance, and the author wants to give the reader a quick background for better understanding of what they are about to read.

An epilogue would come at the end of the book and would add things that have happened since the main part of the book was written. It may be added to a second edition of a biography when the person is still living or to explain how the person's influence is still continuing after his or her death.

## Footnotes, Endnotes and Bibliography

We will not go into detail on this subject or explain exactly how to do these special items. If you want a book that will be "proper" and scholarly, and you have done research that includes quotations by others, you will want to include either footnotes or endnotes and a bibliography. The important thing is to give proper credit to other writers. And as C. Peter Wagner told me, "Remember the copyright rule – COPY RIGHT."

I used footnotes, endnotes and bibliographies in at least two of my books, but most of my books now are smaller, from my heart, and from my own study of the Word. If I want to quote someone, I'll just include the most important credits in the text.

Footnotes are information details recorded at the bottom of the page. They usually are numbered with a small number that matches a number at the end of a quote in the body of the page. Endnotes are similar, but are not placed at the bottom of the page, but rather at the end of the chapter or the book. Endnotes also use a numbering system that matches notes with the quote in the chapter.

If you want your book to be used as a textbook or resource book of some kind, then you can check a reference book out of your library, find instructions on the internet, or just look at some other text books or books by Dr. C. Peter Wagner or other scholars who write more formally and professionally as educators. You can follow these patterns to let the readers know exactly where your information was gleaned.

## Promotional Information

At the back of this book you will find some photos and information about my other books. This is an inexpensive way to inform people of what you have written, or what others, who are associated with you or your ministry, have written.

You can promote ministries, activities such as annual conferences, mission's endeavors, or almost anything that takes place on a regular basis. You can also include your website and email addresses and as much contact information as you think it wise to give out.

## Photos

Adding a photo section in the center of your book is a good way to get people's interest, especially if you telling a story with your book. Pictures make the stories come to life and allow the reader to identify the characters with real faces.

The negative side is that photos cannot usually be done in high quality resolution with the type of print-on-demand digital printing that I normally use. For quality printing, you would probably have to go to an offset press printer. That requires you to invest in a minimum number of books, which is something a beginning author might want to avoid.

If price is not a big concern, and you feel like you already have a fairly large market awaiting you when you publish, you can negotiate a deal with a printer/publisher. You will want to shop around and compare prices and options. Many people have had to buy thousands of their own books, which they end up giving away or storing in their basement or garage.

An example of Digital printing is located in the back of this book, which shows my currently published books. At this point, digital printing meets my needs. However, there will be other books forthcoming, to which I will contribute, that will tell the stories of revival and will require better photos.

This is your book and you can add other things that are

less common if you like. There is no "law" that says you have to follow a certain pattern. These are the normal, but you can be as creative as you would like with your own book. However, if you are unknown in the literary world and the world in general, you might want to focus on doing the basics well before getting too creative.

Now it's time to go to the next step. Getting the content right has been a challenge, but we're not finished yet. We still don't have that book in our hands or the hands of anyone else. Let's finish strong.

# Chapter Six

# From Computer Copy to Beautiful Book

*L*et's assume that you are writing because God has inspired you to do it. Your book is already in the "Future Time" Library of Heaven, and you want to transfer it to the library room storing "Already Published on Earth" books.

You have done considerable research, gathered your information, followed the guidelines we have suggested and finally completed the manuscript. It has some great information and revelation, but it still is not a book.

### Polishing Your Content – Proofing and/or Editing

You may be a great writer and typist. You may be an expert in English grammar and spelling. But once your book gets printed you will find some obvious mistakes. If you are not that great with grammar, etc., you especially need to take a serious look at what you have written.

When I sit down at my computer to continue writing my

book, I usually read what I have written the day or week or month before to help keep the flow going. While I read what I've recently written, I find mistakes or awkward sentence structure. In other words, I edit as I go.

But again, God has blessed me with someone on our volunteer team who is an amazing proofreader. Thanks Carole for all that you do. She has blessed me with her wonderful gift. She finds more little mistakes than I would have ever imagined, and she also finds more awkward sentence structures, etc. I am so much more confident now that people will find very few mistakes as they read my books.

If you don't have anyone in your circle of friends and family who is good with English grammar, etc., you can probably hire someone to do it for you. The print-on-demand publishers (which we will talk about later) often offer editing services for an extra fee.

Cleaning up the little mistakes may seem unimportant, but when you think about the purpose for your book and the high calling of being a spokesperson for Heaven, you will want to do your best. So read and reread what you have written. Make sure it flows smoothly and correct every mistake you can find. Then find someone else who will read it and find the mistakes that you have missed.

## Printing Your Manuscript

If this is your first book, it would be a good idea to print up several copies of the manuscript. You can then give a hard copy to some of the people from whom you would like to receive input. You can print one or two copies on your computer printer and then have copies with plastic covers made and assembled at an office supply store like Staples or Kinkos.

Some of your friends, potential endorsers or foreword writers may be happy to read a computer email attachment and respond to you. However, most people find it easier to read a hard copy that they can take with them and read in their spare time, especially when they can't be near a computer. It is worth the effort to give them your book in the form that they prefer.

The manuscript should have a title page with the same information that will be on the book title page. Of course it probably won't have the finished graphics yet, which may include photos or drawings along with the script, but it will have the title, subtitle and the author's name.

## The Perfect Cover

As you have probably heard, "You can't judge a book by its cover." But it is equally true, "You CAN SELL a book by its cover." You don't want to underestimate the power of an attractive cover. A cover is designed to "attract" the eye.

In a world of thousands of new books published month after month, you want your book to attract the readers who will benefit the most from what you have written. The title is a very important entity, like a painting, but the cover of your book is the frame for your title and your name.

In other words, devote enough time and energy to making the cover as attractive as you possibly can. The content is the heart of the book, but beauty is only skin deep. If the "skin" doesn't attract the reader, then they will probably never get to the heart of your book.

Your printer/publisher may produce your book cover for you, but you don't have to approve a cover that doesn't give your book the look you want. In my current arrangement, my friend, Jeff Doles, formats my content and my covers. For almost every book cover, I have chosen a photo from the photo library of another friend, Robert Bartow, who produces incredible prophetic artwork by combining different photos on his computer.

I choose the photo, and with Robert's permission, I send it to Jeff, who then designs the cover around the photo. Jeff's work is amazing, and I feel so blessed when I look at my book covers. Every book has the power to attract the eye.

## The Final Step – Publishing Your Book

When I wrote my first two books, I didn't have the advantages that I have today. I didn't know where to start or to whom to turn. I found a pastor who was also a printer who said he could print my books for me. I had my artistic sister find some photos that were available to use for a cover. I was pretty proud of the fact that I had two books printed, but they were pretty primitive compared to what I have today. The books were bound with staples, rather than the "perfect" binding used on normal paperback books.

So what do you do if you don't know how to choose your cover and a company to print your book? First, pray that God will lead you to someone who can help you. If you have been a person that loves people and invests in others, God has probably blessed you with some good relationships already.

Most likely, someone you already know has some knowledge or information that can help you. But if you don't yet have the people with the creative and technical skills, your best bet may be to go to a print-on-demand publisher as I did for my third, fourth, fifth and sixth books. They can do a great job and offer you a choice of programs.

I don't want to promote any particular Christian or secular printer/publisher, but you can find almost any information you want on the internet. Through these publishers, you can still own the rights to your book, and they will make it available to the book wholesalers throughout the nation and world, if you chose the right programs.

You can get your books at roughly half of the retail price, depending on the program you choose. These publishers will usually set the retail price for you, and they will continue to make money on every book you buy. The cost of the setup can vary from a few hundred dollars to a couple of thousand dollars, depending on the benefits you choose. Production may take several months after you give them your manuscript, as opposed to bigger publishers, which may take a year or more to edit and print your book.

One of the things the print-on-demand publisher will do for you is purchase and assign your book an ISBN number, which will be used for listing your book in all catalogues and lists of new books. Bookstores that want your book will use this number to purchase it.

If you like a challenge, and are quite computer literate, you might want to consider purchasing your own publishing software and doing your book covers and layout on your own. That is what my friend and setup man, Jeff Doles, does for his own books and CDs.

After using a Christian print-on-demand, self-publishing company, I discovered that Jeff's books were printed by the same printing company that did my books, and apparently he even uses the same software. At any rate, Jeff's work is amazing and he now is doing the same thing for others.

One of the greatest things about working with Jeff, besides the better price, is the fact that he can get the book completed and into my hands in a very short period of time. I have often let him know that I'm trying to get a new book ready for a major conference where it will have the greatest exposure, and he has gone out of his way to help me get it done in time. This is something that probably won't happen with a company that doesn't know you personally. It certainly didn't happen for me.

When you get to this stage of the process, you can get pretty excited. As I shared earlier in the title and the first chapter, I sometimes compare it to giving birth to a baby. For a while, you're not sure what it's going to look like, but you know it's within you. Then there is a lot of labor which culminates in a beautiful product that comes forth from you. It will be something you want everyone to see and appreciate, similar to having a real baby.

Of course, you didn't write the book just to hold one in your hands. You want your book to impact your world. In the next chapter we will examine some of the ways that you can do just that.

## Chapter Seven

# Getting Your Book Into the Marketplace

When your beautiful baby – your new book – is finally in your own hands, you will want to savor the moment and look through it, making sure there are no problems with the publication. You might even want to read it again and feel the passion of what you have written.

After you have thoroughly enjoyed your little time of personal pleasure and fulfillment, you still have another challenge awaiting you. The book is clearly complete and in your hands, but what will you have to do to get it into the hands of others?

If you made a contract with a publisher, your publisher will probably do a lot of the promotion, depending on how much is at stake for them. They are in business to make a profit, even if they have a heart for ministry. But if they have little to gain from your sales, and more to gain from the actual setup process, they will be more interested in finding more authors to publish.

For instance, if your publisher is a print-on-demand company that produces hundreds or thousands of books per year, they probably won't give your book that much special attention. Bigger publishers, on the other hand, print only a handful of books per year, and they highly promote those books because they have invested so much money into the production process.

If you actually do your own layout and setup with your own publishing software, you are basically on your own as far as promotion is concerned. If you really believe you have something that will make a difference in the lives of your readers, you will want to look into all of the promotional possibilities.

The following are some ideas that could help you whether you have a publisher working on your behalf or not. You can decide which of these will work for you.

## Give Away as Many Books as You Can

As Christians, we know that before you reap, you must sow. The very best way to make your book known is to get it into the hands of other people by giving away as many copies as you can, and there are two ways to do this.

The first way, which I do NOT recommend, is to give strategically. That is, give your books to only those whom you think would help you sell your books. They would be people with lots of power and a great sphere of influence.

The other way, which I DO recommend, is to give to those you think would personally benefit. This would include isolated workers on the mission field, people living on fixed income without much education, etc. Whatever your book is about, give it to those that would love to read it and can't afford to buy it, as well as leaders who need the information you have written.

I understand that you have to pay for your books, and you may have to pay more than I do for each book. You may have to limit your giving according to your finances. The main thing is that you give out of love, more than out of personal ambition.

It may be very difficult to keep your heart pure at this stage, but it is important to remember your goal and purpose for writing. It would be good to reread the first chapters of this manual at this point. Getting your book out for the right purpose is very important if you want God to be working with you every step the way.

We don't want to start in the Spirit and finish in the flesh. A good way to guard your heart is to keep giving to those who can't give back to you. You may end up with some awesome testimonies that will bless you more than money in the bank. I just got one of those from the mission field a few days ago.

A young man apprenticing in South Africa saw one of my books that I had given to the African evangelist he was working with. The book's title, *Catching Up to the Third World*, caught his attention. He read it and then emailed me to tell me how much it had stirred his spirit. He found himself saying "YES!!!" over and over again. It didn't result in immediate book sales, but wherever this young man goes, if he sees a book with my name on it, that book will catch his attention. Ultimately, what you sow you will reap. If enough people are blessed by books with your name on them, then other people will hear about your books, which translates into future sales. As we said before, the key is that the content inside the book must meet a need and touch a chord in the heart of the reader. If that happens, and you give away enough books, good things will happen to you also.

## Internet Opportunities

The greatest potential exposure for your books could very well be the World Wide Web because there are so many ways to use the internet today. First of all, you can start your own website if you don't already have one. Not being a web expert myself, I rely upon the help and wisdom of others to help me with my own site.

Networking with other websites is another way to expand your opportunities. You can ask other friends and associates who have their own sites to add a link to your site, and you should of course offer to provide a link to their site at the same time. It should be a win/win situation if they believe in you and you believe in them.

Another way to use the internet is to get your books turned into e-books. For a price, people can download your book and read it without having to buy a hard copy. You will still get royalties transferred to your account from your e-book sales.

Having your books promoted on a major Christian mailing list service is another very effective way to inform people about your book. The Elijah List is one of the largest mailing list services in the Christian world, and if they will promote your book, you may have very good results. Of course, every Christian author has the same ambition for recognition that you do, and it may be a real challenge to get someone there to actually look at your book, unless you are already known by their staff.

There are other ways to take advantage of the internet, but you would be well advised to find an expert on the subject and consult with them. It may cost you something, but it may be a wise investment.

## Paid Advertising

This may or may not be a wise option. My brief experience tells me that it can be a waste of good money. However, if you have an overall plan and strategy and know your target audience, you can probably make it work well to your advantage.

You can advertise in various magazines, periodicals and publications, or ads can be put on radio or TV as well. If you have plenty of resources to put into the effort, the cost of advertising could possibly pay for itself in book sales, and your message will reach more people, regardless of the profit or loss financially.

## Free Publicity

There are many radio and television stations, both Christian and secular, hosting talk shows that love to interview authors. Often, they will offer your book for a donation to the program. They may even buy your book in bulk amounts, and you can get the word out and sell some books at the same time.

Being in the kind of faith ministry we are, we do little personal promotion of any kind unless someone invites us to be on radio or television. Some of it has been productive, while other experiences have seemed to produce almost no tangible results. We simply trust God and go through the doors that He opens. God does the rest.

## Working with Book Stores

If you have time and feel led to do so, you can visit Christian or secular bookstores and show them your book. You can offer to do a book signing if they are willing to give you a table to sign your book. Some stores have a special little section for local writers and will be willing to work with you. Your sales may not make you a lot of money, but little by little your book will be seen by more people.

Along with the major bookstores, you might want to approach some of the larger churches that have bookstores in their facilities. You might find them very interested, especially if you are from their local area.

## Hiring an Agency to Promote your Book

There are plenty of agencies out there that will take your money and promise to get your book noticed by bookstores and even movie writers. Again, you can find almost anything you want on the internet, including book promotional agencies. Usually, they want somewhere between $500.00 and

$2,000.00 for various promotional packages, but they do not guarantee any results for your money.

There are agencies that may even call you or send you ads in the mail or by email. I received such a call at home, and I asked the agency's salesperson if they had any programs that were based on the actual results. I wanted them to be profit-motivated, so that they would be more aggressive in promoting the book. The salesperson responded that they didn't work that way. Since I didn't have any money to risk, I declined the offer.

## Conference Book Tables

Frankly, most of our sales come from our own meetings. If you have a traveling ministry, you have an automatic outlet for your ministry products.

In addition, you may have opportunities to get your books on the tables at conferences where you are not a speaker or host. We have people that order our books from all over the country to put on their book tables at their conferences. Of course, we are delighted to do so.

The list of ways to get your books into the hands of other people could go on and on. The most important thing is to be alert to the prompting of the Holy Spirit. He will tell you when the door is open to someone's heart. Always be ready to give away a book to someone who could benefit from it.

I like to keep a box of books in my car trunk. When I meet someone I ask the Lord if they could use one of my books. When I attend other conferences for my own benefit, I usually give away many books to people I meet. Sometimes

I hear back from people a full year or more later, and they express great appreciation for the message and motivation that they received from the book.

Well, it seems that we are done, but wait a minute. I think there's one more thing that we should mention at this point. If you really want to be a known author and impact your world, you probably need to go beyond all the information we have discussed so far. Let's go to the next important step.

## Chapter Eight

# One Last Little Thing

How exciting it is to get your own book in your hand! It has your own name on it and you know it is God's gift to you and God's gift to others. It seems your dream has been fulfilled! You have even figured out how to get your book out into the marketplace, and you are being blessed with testimonies from people who are getting blessed every day.

What could be more exciting than that? But let me challenge you at this point with the thought that perhaps you have only just begun. Yes, that's right! If you have done it once, it is so much easier to do it again.

Not only is it easier, but you already have a readership following. If your readers liked the first book, they will be looking forward to the second one and then the third.

Every book gets easier to do. Your typing should have improved, and your skills will all be getting better and better.

You have found the people who can help you with things

you are not very good at, and you have their contact information stored in your telephone or computer. It just gets easier and easier and you just might become addicted.

Of course, you need to have something to write about. But my experience is that if you were given one revelation or message to share, and you are faithful with that one, God will give you more. If He called you to write one book, He will probably call you to write another one.

When I started writing at the age of about fifty-three, I knew that I would be writing more than one book. I thought to myself, "I'll just keep writing books until one of them takes off." I knew it might take time to become known well enough to make a big impact, but I felt that if I kept at it, there would eventually be a great reward.

This is book number thirteen for me, and as I stated above, every book gets easier. I learn to major on the majors and minor on the minors. What I shared in the earlier chapters is wisdom gained from experience. You now can build on the experiences of others like myself and add your own insights.

Then don't be surprised when people begin to ask you how to write and publish the book that's within them. You may also be considerably younger than I am by the time you begin to mentor and teach others the writing skills you have learned from your own experience.

Now, let's wrap up this little book.

You can be an author within a matter of months. If you started today, you could possibly produce your book by some target date that means a lot to you, whether it's Christmas, your birthday, your spouse's birthday or some conference or convention.

Start with vision, passion and a strong desire to make a difference. Follow that up with some research, organization and then writing. Learn to use the computer software, and edit as you go, making it flow more and more smoothly. Stay on track and avoid the ever-inviting bunny trails.

Get the help you need for proofing, editing and publishing and before long you will have the book in your hands. Like having a baby, you are a proud papa or mama of a brand new book.

You also know that you have done it all by the grace of God and for His glory. He has been with you all the way. He gave you the revelation, the creativity and all the gifts that went into the production of your book. He deserves the worship, the honor and all the glory. Make sure you give it to Him!

But is your book in the Library Rooms of Heaven? If you were privileged to visit Heaven, would you find your own book there?

I believe that God led you to this book. I believe that if your spirit was stirred when we shared about the library rooms of Heaven, then you are quite probably one of those whom God has given a mandate to speak His words on paper and release them on the earth. It will be another case of Heaven invading earth, as our friend, Bill Johnson, teaches so eloquently in his own book *When Heaven Invades Earth*.

If you do write a book that has been prepared in Heaven, then surely God will help you every step of the way. His grace is upon you and His Spirit inhabits you. Rebuke the spirit of fear. Receive and appropriate the Spirit of Power, the Spirit of Love, and the Spirit of a Sound Mind. These are the gifts that God has given you. (II Timothy 1:7)

If God is for you, who can possibly stand against you? Every obstacle will be overcome. The enemy cannot stop you. Neither lack of time or skill can keep your book from becoming a reality.

Trust God for His perfect timing to complete each project in the process. You are co-creating with the Living God. It doesn't all depend on you. You depend totally on Him. When you wait on Him, He will renew your strength. You will run and not grow weary; you will walk and not faint.

Rather than failing and quitting, you will actually soar like an eagle. You will rise up and be carried up on the winds of the Holy Spirit. You will see things you have never seen before because you will have eagle eyes - the eyes that see what is not visible to the human eye.

Be with Him and He will be with you. Your writing will be a blessing to Him, to others and to you. It will surely be worth the effort. You can give birth to your brand new "baby", even if you are older than Sarah!

Are you ready? Can you see your book in your mind? May God open your eyes to see it! May your heart pant for it for His glory and honor!

May God bless this incredible journey with the discovery of the wonderful treasure, which you have hunted for and have not yet found. And may your readers discover the treasure revealed through your writing that will change and bless their lives forever!

Jesus is with you! YOU CAN DO IT!!!

# BEN R. PETERS

With over 35 years of ministry experience, Ben Peters with his wife, Brenda, have been called to an international apostolic ministry of equipping and activating others. As founders and directors of Open Heart Ministries, Ben and Brenda have ministered to tens of thousands with teaching and prophetic ministry. The result is that many have been saved, healed and delivered and activated into powerful ministries of their own.

Ben has been given significant insights for the body of Christ and has written eleven books in the past five years, since beginning a full-time itinerant ministry. His passions and insights include unity in the body of Christ, accessing the glory of God, five-fold team ministry, prophetic ministry, and signs and wonders for the world-wide harvest.

The Peters not only minister at churches, camps, retreats and conferences, but also host numerous conferences with cutting-edge apostolic and prophetic leaders. They reside now in Northern Illinois with the youngest two of their five children, and travel extensively internationally.

Open Heart Ministries
www.ohmint.org
benrpeters@juno.com
15648 Bombay Blvd.
S. Beloit, IL 61080

**Holy Passion: Desire on Fire**
Igniting the Torch of Godly Passion
by Ben R. Peters

Available from Open Heart Ministries
www.ohmint.org

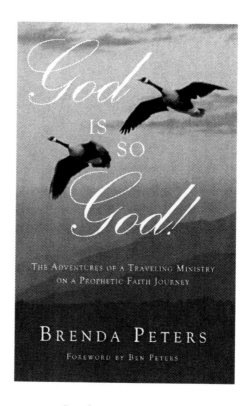

**God Is So God!**
The Adventures of a Traveling Ministry
on a Prophetic Faith Journey
by Brenda Peters

Available from Open Heart Ministries
www.ohmint.org

**Signs and Wonders**
To Seek or Not to Seek
by Ben R. Peters

Available from Open Heart Ministries
www.ohmint.org

## With Me
A Captivating Journey Into Intimacy
by Ben R. Peters

Available from Open Heart Ministries
www.ohmint.org

**Resurrection!**
A Manual for Raising the Dead
by Ben R. Peters

Available from Open Heart Ministries
www.ohmint.org

**Prophetic Ministry**
Strategic Key to the Harvest
by Ben R. Peters

Available from Open Heart Ministries
www.ohmint.org

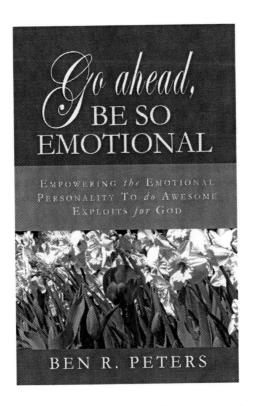

## Go Ahead, Be So Emotional
Empowering the Emotional Personality
to do Awesome Exploits for God
by Ben R. Peters

Available from Open Heart Ministries
www.ohmint.org

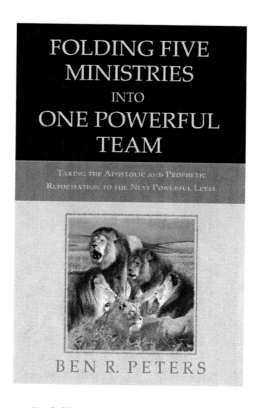

## Folding Five Ministries
## Into One Powerful Team
Taking the Apostolic and Prophetic Reformation
to the Next Powerful Level
by Ben R. Peters

Available from Open Heart Ministries
www.ohmint.org

## Catching up to the Third World
Seven Indispensable Keys
To EXPLOSIVE Revival
in the Western Church
by Ben R. Peters

Available from Open Heart Ministries
www.ohmint.org

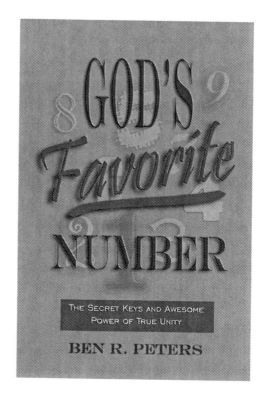

**God's Favorite Number**
The Secret Keys and Awesome
Power of True Unity
by Ben R. Peters

Available from Open Heart Ministries
www.ohmint.org

**The Skin & the Skeleton**
What to Do When the Laid-Back
Marries the Up-Set
by Ken Peters

Available from Open Heart Ministries
www.ohmint.org

Printed in the United States
149638LV00004B/4/A

9 780978 988425